MAJOR WORLD RELIGIONS

hinduism

Major World Religions

Buddhism

Christianity

Hinduism

Islam

Judaism

Sikhism

MAJOR WORLD RELIGIONS

hinduism

Nalini Rangan

MASON CREST
PHILADELPHIA

Mason Crest
450 Parkway Drive, Suite D
Broomall, PA 19008
www.masoncrest.com

©2018 by Mason Crest, an imprint of National Highlights, Inc.

Printed and bound in the United States of America.

CPSIA Compliance Information: Batch #MWR2017.
For further information, contact Mason Crest at 1-866-MCP-Book.

First printing
1 3 5 7 9 8 6 4 2

Library of Congress Cataloging-in-Publication Data

on file at the Library of Congress
ISBN: 978-1-4222-3818-9 (hc)
ISBN: 978-1-4222-7971-7 (ebook)

Major World Religions series ISBN: 978-1-4222-3815-8

QR CODES AND LINKS TO THIRD-PARTY CONTENT

Table of Contents

KEY ICONS TO LOOK FOR:

Words to understand: These words with their easy-to-understand definitions will increase the reader's understanding of the text while building vocabulary skills.

Sidebars: This boxed material within the main text allows readers to build knowledge, gain insights, explore possibilities, and broaden their perspectives by weaving together additional information to provide realistic and holistic perspectives.

Educational Videos: Readers can view videos by scanning our QR codes, providing them with additional educational content to supplement the text. Examples include news coverage, moments in history, speeches, iconic sports moments and much more!

Text-dependent questions: These questions send the reader back to the text for more careful attention to the evidence presented there.

Research projects: Readers are pointed toward areas of further inquiry connected to each chapter. Suggestions are provided for projects that encourage deeper research and analysis.

Series glossary of key terms: This back-of-the book glossary contains terminology used throughout this series. Words found here increase the reader's ability to read and comprehend higher-level books and articles in this field.

Hindu pilgrims to the sacred city of Varanasi in northern India set small lamps, called diyas, afloat on the sacred Ganges River.

 # Words to Understand in This Chapter

atma—the self: body, mind, or spirit; or the Supreme Spirit.

Brahma—the first created being, created by Vishnu; the grandfather of the universe, member of the Hindu trinity.

deva—a divine being; the higher order of created being.

karma—action; past actions, which accrue results; hence can refer to the results of past actions.

Paramatma—the supreme self, or supersoul, who dwells within every living being.

reincarnation—being reborn in a new body.

samsara—the seemingly endless cycle of birth, old age, disease, and death.

Shiva—the form of God who dissolves the universe with his dance in a circle of fire.

Vishnu—preserver of the Universe, who creates the universe from his breath, and Brahma, the first living being.

ॐ

1 What Do Hindus Believe?

The word "Hindu" comes from the River Sindhu, or Indus, which flows across the northwest plains of India. Invaders who crossed the river named the land and the people after the river. A more accurate name for Hinduism is *Sanatan Dharma*, which means "the eternal truth of life."

Sanatan dharma describes the essential quality that unites all living things—human, animal, and vegetable—with the universe that surrounds them and, ultimately, with God, the source of their existence. It is the belief in the unity of all life that causes Hindus to resist separating their own faith from the other great faith traditions of the world. To a Hindu, all religions are part of the process of discovering the unity of God, humanity, and nature.

A Hindu man meditates near the holy city of Varanasi. For Hindus, the ultimate purpose of life is to understand God.

At the heart of Hinduism is a belief in an eternal spiritual truth, called Brahman, from whom all existence comes. The purpose of life, Hindus say, is to understand this truth and to understand our own spiritual identity as the eternal *atma*, or soul.

Hindus believe that the soul is eternal and lives many lifetimes, in one body after another. Being reborn in a new body is called *reincarnation*. The soul is sometimes born in

a human body, sometimes in an animal body, and sometimes in a plant body, such as a tree. Only human life, however, offers the chance for the *atma* to learn the eternal
spiritual truth. Therefore, Hindus believe that it is important to use the opportunity of a human birth to understand
who we are, and who God is. In this way, we can end the
cycle of reincarnation and be reunited with the eternal spiritual reality, or God.

*A funeral ceremony on the banks of the Ganges River near Varanasi. Hindus believe that
each soul (atma) is reincarnated in another form after death, until the soul achieves the
eternal spiritual truth.*

The cycle of rebirth is called *samsara*. It gives rise to the basic problems of material life, which are birth, disease, old age, and death.

Karma in Action

Karma is the Sanskrit word for "action." Actions are important because they produce reactions. Hindus believe that everything that we experience, pleasant or unpleasant, is linked to our past actions in this lifetime or in some previous lifetime, whether or not we see the connections. This does not mean there is no free choice, because we can choose to change our actions, and so change our future. Belief in karma teaches us to accept responsibility for our behavior, and learn from our mistakes.

Under the influence of karma, the soul moves upward and downward on the wheel of rebirth. Hinduism teaches that the ultimate solution to life's basic problems is to be released from your karma, and gain freedom from the cycle of birth and rebirth.

One Truth, Many Deities

Hindus believe in one "supreme truth," which manifests itself in many forms. God exists as the original creator of the universe, as its maintainer, and as its ultimate destroyer. These three functions are personified in the deities of *Brahma* the Creator, Vishnu the Preserver, and Shiva the Destroyer. Another important aspect of the supreme truth is the goddess Devi, who appears in different forms to accompany the different aspects of God.

According to Hindu philosophy, the things a person does every day—whether good or bad—will effect the position of the atma on the cycle of rebirth.

Members of the Tamil tribe in Malaysia participate in a ceremony for Murugan, a Hindu war deity. Indian Hindus refer to the god as Karthikeya.

The supreme truth is revered in the hearts of all living beings as the "supersoul," called *Paramatma*.

Vishnu enters the human world in every age to teach us the path of religion and to show his love. Vishnu's incarnations as Rama and as Krishna are particularly important to Hindus.

Besides these primary forms of God, there are other divine forms, called *devas* (or demigods), empowered by God to govern the forces of nature, such as the planets and the elements. Examples include Agni, the god of fire; Vayu, god of the wind; Surya, god of the sun; and the goddess Ganga, spirit of the Ganges River. Hindus honor God directly, in the personal forms of Krishna, Rama, Vishnu, and Shiva, or indirectly by honoring the divine forms of nature, such as fire, wind, and sun.

There are many stories about the Hindu gods and other important figures. These stories are important because they impart the traditional wisdom embedded in them. Stories are easier to remember than sermons or philosophy, but can be just as profound. They are accessible to everyone

A Nadarajah statue represents Shiva in his role as lord of the cosmic dance. The god is holding fire in his left hand, and a snake in his right. Hindus believe that at the end of time, the universe will be destroyed through Shiva's dance.

Educational Video

For a short video of Hindu creation stories, scan here:

because they can be communicated by song, drama, or dance, and have a big influence on their audience.

One of the most powerful Hindu stories is the epic Ramayana, about how Rama rescued his wife Sita, and dedicated himself to the good of his people. Another joyful and profound story is of Krishna, who lived in the forest as a cowherd in his youth and later became a prince. Krishna taught the Bhagavad Gita, perhaps the best summary of Hindu teachings.

A Young Hindu's Life Today

Sanjay Chandaria, who is 15, and his sister Anita, 17, live with their parents in New Jersey. Their grandmother, who also lives with the family, goes a Hindu temple every day, and has taught Sanjay and Anita all they know about the Hindu religion. In the following paragraphs, he describes how he practices his faith in his daily life:

"My father came to the United States in 1996. He is an engineer and had qualified for a H-1B visa, which allowed him to work and live in the United States for up to six years. He later applied to become a U.S. citizen, which allowed him to bring his mother—my grandmother—to this country. When he married my mother, he brought her to the U.S. as well.

"My grandmother exercises her matriarchal influence over our home. She made sure my sisters and I were brought up as vegetarians and taught about Hinduism, by telling us stories when we were little, and teaching us songs to sing at the temple.

"I like going to the temple. I can meet my friends there and we all get along. I also have other friends, from other parts of the community, because people in the United States enjoy a very multicultural life. There are lots of opportunities to meet people at school and college, and around the city.

The Shri Swaminarayan temple in Robbinsville, New Jersey, where Sanjay's family attends services.

Sanjay Chandaria is a typical American teenager.

"When I finish my studies, I hope to go into partnership with some of my friends to start our own business. I want to do business because it's something I have a natural talent for. It's my family tradition to be merchants. If I'm successful, I will use my money to support the community. I also want to travel to Gujarat, in India, to see the village that my family originally came from.

"My sister, Anita, wants to be a lawyer. She strongly believes in people's right to freedom. People should not be made to suffer from other people's prejudice, she says, as our parents suffered when they first arrived from East Africa. They now consider themselves lucky to be living in a free society. That is why Anita wants to work as a lawyer. There are so many rights we must protect, she says.

"To be successful in life, you have to believe in what you are doing, and make yourself your own message by setting a good example. I think my Hindu faith has influenced my views, because I was brought up with a clear moral code that I believe in. But I do not expect everyone to be like me. Hinduism is very open-minded and accepts people the way they are. It has taught me to respect all people and to see all religions as paths to the same ultimate truth.

 Text-Dependent Questions

1. What does the Sanskrit word *karma* mean?
2. What three Hindu deities personified the concept of the "supreme truth?"
3. What deity is Krishna considered an incarnation of?

 Research Project

Using the Internet or your school library, do some research to answer the question "Should we believe in an eternal spiritual reality?" Those who agree will note that throughout history, humans have chosen to believe in a spiritual reality beyond this world. Just because we cannot see or hear something, does not mean it does not exist. It is reasonable to believe in other forms of existence besides our own. Those who disagree with this perspective believe that there is no proof of a spiritual existence. People should just believe in what they can see, and religion is just an escape from reality, they would likely argue. Present your conclusion in a two-page report, providing examples from your research that support your answer.

 ## Words to Understand in This Chapter

caste—rigid division of Hindu society, often leading to discrimination.

dharma—an essential quality that unites all beings with the universe and with God.

guru—a teacher of Hinduism, in the traditional "disciplic succession" system.

mukti—salvation; liberation from the ties of karma and the cycle of rebirth.

varna—the four main divisions of Hindu society.

Veda—spiritual knowledge; the ancient Sanskrit hymns directly revealed by God.

The excavated ruins of Mohenjo-daro, an ancient city of the Indus Valley civilization that was built around 2600 BCE and flourished until 1900 BCE. The city was rediscovered in the 1920s. Hinduism originated in the Indus River valley thousands of years ago.

2 The Origins of Hinduism

The Indian Subcontinent is home to one of the world's oldest civilizations. About 4,600 years ago, in and around the region of the Indus River valley (in present-day Pakistan and western India), cities and towns connected through a well-organized trade network and, probably, political alliances, grew up where some of the earliest farming and herding communities had been established nearly two millennia before. Archaeologists have labeled the peoples who constructed, inhabited, and governed these urban centers the Indus Valley civilization or the Harappan culture (after Harappa, the town where evidence of the civilization was first uncovered).

The Indus Valley civilization extended across a huge area of at least 250,000 square miles (650,000 sq km), approximately the size of California and Wyoming com-

The archaeological site of Harappa, a city near the Ravi River in modern-day Pakistan that was settled around 2600 BCE. It was one of the largest cities in ancient India. The Bronze Age civilizations of the Indus River Valley are sometimes known as the Harappan civilization or culture, after this important city.

bined. Its cities—which are carefully laid out with east-west and north-south boulevards and which frequently have extensive drainage systems for removing sewage—show a high degree of planning and organization. Archaeologists believe that, in addition to the widespread commerce within its territory, the Indus Valley civilization also traded with cultures in Mesopotamia (modern-day Iraq), the Persian Gulf, and Central Asia.

For some seven centuries, the urban centers of the Indus Valley civilization remained highly integrated and culturally cohesive. Sometime around 1900 BCE, however, this unification began to give way to regional fragmentation. Archaeologists today believe that the Indus Valley civilization did not disappear abruptly in the face of an invasion by outsiders, as had been theorized by earlier scholars. Rather, the once-unified culture is now thought to have evolved in distinct directions in different areas, surviving until perhaps 1300 to 1000 BCE.

Modern scholars disagree on how Hinduism arose in India. Some scholars believe that Indo-Aryan groups gradually migrated from Central Asia, and that these groups created the Vedic culture. (This term comes from the *Vedas*, sacred texts that contain the essential truths of Hinduism.) Others argue that Hinduism developed from the cultural exchange that took place when the migrating Indo-Aryans came into contact with Dravidian groups already residing in the Indian Subcontinent. Still other specialists insist that Vedic culture evolved over many centuries entirely from within the Subcontinent (some even positing that Indo-Aryan groups actually originated in northwestern India and later migrated to Central Asia and Europe).

Ancient Traditions

The origins of Hinduism stretch back beyond the beginnings of recorded history. The traditions and teachings of Hinduism were passed down orally from one generation to the next, until they began to be written down in their present Sanskrit form during the second millennium BCE. According to these ancient traditions, Krishna lived around

The Sacred Language

Sanskrit is an ancient language of India. This language was used to write the important scriptures of Hinduism, such as the four Vedas. Sanskrit is written using an alphabet called Devanagari, which means "the language of the gods." Hindus believe that Sanskrit is written and spoken by the *devas*, who live in heavenly realms above the earth. Although the Hindu scriptures are translated into other languages besides Sanskrit, anyone who wants to study them intensely learns Sanskrit. The best-known Sanskrit word is *Om*, meaning "Supreme Truth."

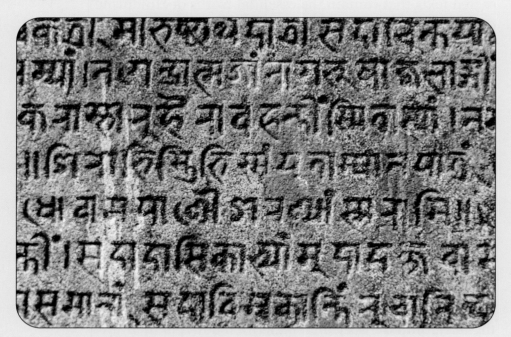

An ancient Sanskrit text etched into a stone tablet.

3000 BCE, and Rama lived tens of thousands of years before Krishna.

The early teachings of Hinduism were recorded in verse form, so that they could more easily be committed to memory. Early Hindu teachers thought dependence on writing was a sign of weak memory. They preferred to memorize everything and taught their disciples in the same way. The early hymns were collected into four groups, the Rig, Sama, Yajur, and Atharva, which together are called the four Vedas.

Educational Video

To hear a standard Hindu prayer, scan here:

The Rig-Veda, the longest, oldest, and most important of the Vedas, contains more than 1,000 hymns dedicated to a variety of gods. The other Vedas—the Sama-Veda, the Yajur-Veda, and the Atharva-Veda—include chants and invocations and detail the proper ways to perform various rituals.

Later, other Hindu texts were written. These include the Puranas (the old stories), the Ramayana, and the Mahabharata, which includes the popular Bhagavad Gita.

Differences Between Hinduism and Other Religions

Many Westerners have difficulty understanding Hinduism, and attempts to precisely define the beliefs and practices of

Hinduism can be frustrating. This is mainly due to the fact that Hinduism lacks a central creed, an organized religious hierarchy, or even a unified set of practices accepted by all believers. Rather, Hindus hold a broad range of beliefs and follow a variety of ritual practices. For the most part, Hindus do not seek converts; nor do they claim that theirs is the only path to spiritual truth. In fact, Hinduism has proved highly flexible in adapting to and assimilating a range of influences and ideas; it has thus evolved significantly over the centuries. And Hinduism is not simply a religion; it also represents a way of organizing society, influencing (if not dictating) an individual's social class and career options.

If exact, comprehensive definitions of Hinduism are elusive, some important generalizations can be made. First, Hinduism differs fundamentally from religions such as Judaism, Christianity, and Islam—which are all monotheistic faiths whose adherents believe in a personal God. In Hinduism many gods are worshiped, though all are manifestations of a single, supreme God known as Brahman. Yet it is not accurate to equate "Brahman" with God in the sense that Westerners typically use the word; Brahman is more like an impersonal divine principle that permeates everything—the "oneness" of all that exists. That said, Hindus may—and many Hindus do—revere personal deities.

While Jews, Christians, and Muslims tend to see history in linear terms—with time inclining toward a future point at which God will judge humanity, rewarding the

This detail from a fresco outside the Mehrangarh Fort in the Indian state of Rajasthan depicts a variety of gods from Hindu mythology.

righteous and punishing the wicked—Hindus view time as cyclical. The universe is created, maintained, and then destroyed, only to be created anew in a never-ending cycle. The process takes place under the auspices of three gods or aspects of the divine principle: Brahma (the Creator), Vishnu (the Preserver), and Shiva (the Destroyer).

This conception of the cyclical nature of the universe finds a rough parallel in Hindu beliefs about the individual soul. Most Hindus (unlike their Jewish, Christian, and

Muslim counterparts) believe in reincarnation. Karma determines the station to which a person is born in a successive life. Bad deeds lead to rebirth into a less privileged social position (or even to rebirth as an animal); good actions lead to rebirth into a higher social position. The individual soul travels through many lifetimes as the cycle of *samsara*—birth, life (with all its accompanying misery), death, and

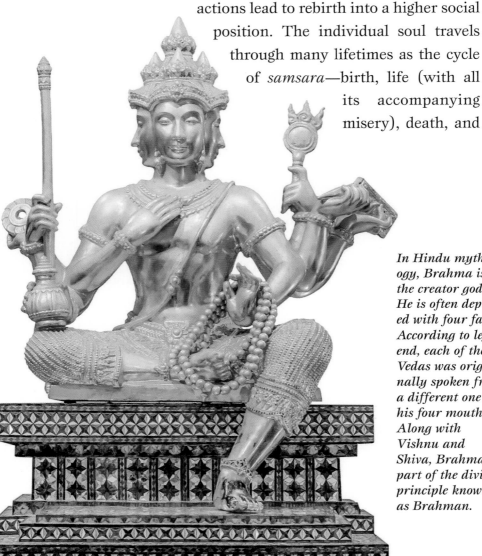

In Hindu mythology, Brahma is the creator god. He is often depicted with four faces. According to legend, each of the Vedas was originally spoken from a different one of his four mouths. Along with Vishnu and Shiva, Brahma is part of the divine principle known as Brahman.

rebirth—is repeated. The ultimate goal, liberation or salvation from *samsara*, is called *moksha* or *mukti*. It marks the individual soul's union with Brahman, which is described as the supreme truth.

Hindus believe that multiple paths can lead toward rebirth into a better life and ultimately to *moksha*, depend-

A statue of Shiva stands outside a Hindu temple in Sri Lanka. Shiva is one of the three deities that make up the divine principle Brahman, as the god of destruction. Shiva is often depicted with a third eye in the middle of his forehead, and his primary weapon is a three-headed spear called a trishula.

The god Krishna kills the demon king Kansa in this scene from the Mahabharata. Krishna is one of the most popular Hindu deities. He is seen as an incarnation, or avatar, of Vishnu, who is one of three major gods that make up the divine principle known as Brahman. In Hindu art, both Krishna and Vishnu are often depicted with blue coloring.

ing on the individual. These include meditation, scrupulous ethical and moral discipline, pursuit of right knowledge and right action, abandonment of attachment to the results of one's actions, elimination of passions, and devotion to a personal deity, particularly Rama or Krishna (incarnations of the god Vishnu).

To the casual Western observer, one of the most striking—and objectionable—aspects of Hinduism is its apparent support of social inequality. The *caste* system of hereditary social classes is central to Hindu beliefs and is deeply ingrained in Indian society. Children are born into their father's caste, and throughout their lives they remain in that caste, which defines their social identity, status, and career choices and even influences whom they may marry and whom their friends may be. There are four main castes—Brahmans (composed of priests, scholars, and teachers), Ksatriyas (warriors, aristocrats, governors), Vaisyas (farmers, merchants, skilled laborers), and Sudras (servants or laborers). Within these four main castes are thousands of subcastes. Strict rules regulate behavior with-

Temple art depicts Rama with a bow and arrows. The Hindu epic Ramayana tells how Rama must rescue his wife from the demon king Ravana. Like Krishna, Rama is often depicted with blue skin, as he is believed to be an avatar for the deity Vishnu.

in and between castes. Breaking these rules can result in being shunned as an outcaste and not belonging to any community. Casteless "untouchables" (now called Dalits) were traditionally forbidden to have any contact with other members of society; it was even thought that touching the shadow of an untouchable would defile a member of a higher caste. In modern times, India has officially abolished "untouchability" and outlawed caste-based discrimination, but caste still influences everyday life.

A low-caste Hindu woman works removing human waste from homes by hand in the state of Haryana, India. Although the modern state does not recognize the caste system, most Hindus are very aware of the historical distinctions between the castes.

Hindus believe that ethical and moral conduct, key to the individual soul's liberation, is determined by the principle of *varna-ashrama-dharma* (*varna* is caste, *dharma* is duty, and *ashrama* is one's stage of life). Righteous conduct lies in doing one's duty in accordance with one's caste and fulfilling the responsibilities associated with different periods of one's life (such as student, householder, or older person). The concept of *varna-ashrama-dharma* maintains order in Hindu society and legitimizes the status quo.

Influences on Hinduism

Throughout history, Hinduism has proved highly flexible, adapting and assimilating beliefs from other religions. The middle part of the first millennium BCE saw the founding of two major faiths that would present challenges to early Hinduism, which emphasized the importance of rituals and sacrifices and was dominated by the concerns of the Brahman priests.

Jainism, founded in northeast India in the sixth century BCE by Mahavira ("the Great Hero"), rejected the caste system, the authority of the Vedas, and certain other Hindu beliefs and practices. Jains emphasize simplicity, good works, and consideration for all life as the path to the soul's liberation from the cycle of birth and rebirth, and they do nothing that may endanger an animal.

Buddhism also rejected the caste system, along with Hinduism's Vedic ritual. It was founded in the latter part of the sixth century BCE by Siddhartha Gautama, known as the Buddha ("Enlightened One"). A wealthy prince from

An ancient statue of the Buddha in Thailand. Siddhartha Gautama is believed to have lived and taught in the eastern part of India between the sixth and fourth centuries BCE.

northern India who renounced the luxuries of palace life, he taught the "four noble truths": existence is sorrow; sorrow arises from earthly attachments; cessation of attachments ends suffering or sorrow; and *nirvana* (release from the cycle of birth and rebirth) can be achieved by following a path of spiritual discipline. Buddhism, as his teachings became known, emphasized the importance of meditation and contemplation.

Hinduism adapted to the spread of Buddhism and Jainism by incorporating Buddhist and Jain practices and beliefs. Vedic rituals and sacrifices became less significant as meditation and contemplation assumed more importance. Many Hindus also adopted the values of nonviolence and concern for animals, including vegetarianism.

This renewed form of Hinduism had emerged by the start of the Gupta Empire (320–550 CE), which united northern India. From their capital Pataliputra (in the present-day Indian state of Bihar), the Gupta rulers presided over a golden age of Hindu culture. Important works of philosophy, poetry, drama, and Sanskrit grammar were written. Art and architecture flourished.

An invasion by Huns from Central Asia eroded the Guptas' power, however. By the early sixth century, their hold on northern India had been loosened, and the region soon fragmented into a host of smaller competing states. A king named Harsha, who came to power in 606 CE, managed to reunite northern India under his strong rule. But at his death in 647, Harsha's kingdom disintegrated, and northern India again slipped into anarchy.

The Arrival of Islam

Around this same time—roughly 650 CE—the Islamic religion is believed to have reached India, brought by seafaring Arabs who traded in the region of Sind (a city in present-day southern Pakistan). In 711, Muslim Arab armies invaded Sind, conquering the Hindu rulers and forcing people to convert to Islam.

In the ninth and tenth centuries, Muslim armies began a series of raids into northwestern India. Under a Turk named Mahmud of Ghazni, the Muslims captured most of the Punjab region. Mahmud was motivated in part by a desire to spread Islam through *jihad*, or "holy war." Known as "the Idol Smasher," he destroyed Hindu idols, artwork, and temples; he also massacred large numbers of "infidel" Hindus. But plunder was probably at least an equally important motive. Mahmud looted gold and jewels and carried thousands of women and slaves back to Ghazni. Among the important Hindu cities Mahmud sacked were Somnath (in the present-day Indian state of Gujarat) and Mathura and Kannauj (both in Uttar Pradesh). By 1026 Mahmud had annexed the Punjab into his empire. After his death four years later, however, Mahmud's successors were unable to maintain control of the region.

During the next few centuries, Muslims continued to make inroads into Hindu lands in India. Invading armies led by such figures as Genghis Khan and Tamerlane tried to conquer India during the thirteenth and fourteenth centuries. In the 1520s, a Muslim warlord named Babur gained control of Lahore and most of the Indian subcontinent. He established the Mughal Empire, which ruled India for hundreds of years.

The Mughal rulers were Muslims, but they had to practice religious tolerance because most people living in the empire were Hindus. However, some rulers were less tolerant than others, so tensions and violence between Hindus and Muslims within the empire were not uncommon.

Around this same time, a new religion evolved in the Punjab region. Sikhs were once Hindus, but were influenced by the teachings of a series of wise men, known as the *gurus*. The gurus taught that all people were equal, and

One of India's most famous architectural sites, the Taj Mahal, was built by a Muslim ruler of the Mughal Empire.

rejected the Hindu caste system. The Sikhs often found themselves fighting against both Hindus and Muslims.

Hinduism in the Modern Day

The modern era of Hinduism began in the eighteenth century, thanks largely to European influences brought to India by the British.

The British Raj, or rule over India, had its roots in a commercial enterprise. On December 31, 1600, the British East India Company, a private corporation, was chartered in London. The English government granted the East India Company monopoly rights on all British trade with India and the Far East. Before the end of the 17th century, the East India Company had firmly established itself on the Subcontinent, acquiring trading rights in Madras (1639), Bombay (1664), and Calcutta (1696).

In many respects India proved an ideal place for the British merchants to do business. Europe craved goods from the East, including silk, china, calico, and tea, and labor in India was cheap—one pence a day versus six back in Britain—so the goods were inexpensive to produce.

In 1744, the British began fighting with the French for control over trade in India. Both sides enlisted Indian rajas as allies. There were many opportunities, as India at the time had about 650 separate princely kingdoms. The British general Robert Clive won a series of battlefield victories, helping to make the British East India Company he richest and most powerful force in the subcontinent.

In 1756, a Muslim ruler in India's Bengal province

attempted to drive out the East India Company. He captured the company's fort in Calcutta. But Clive's forces defeated the Muslims at the Battle of Plassey in June 1857. After this the East India Company began collecting taxes in Bengal, India's most populous region. Soon this function

British soldiers fight against Indian troops during their conquest of the subcontinent. The period of British domination of India began in the early seventeenth century, with the British government officially taking control between 1858 and 1947.

was taken over by the British government, marking the start of British rule over India.

The British soldiers and traders who came to India in the eighteenth and nineteenth centuries were often accompanied by missionaries. The missionaries introduced Christian values and challenged social practices that they found unacceptable. These included child marriage and aspects of the caste system—in particular, the discrimination suffered by the so-called "untouchables." Hindu leaders responded by introducing reforms, many of which were aimed at returning to the basics of Vedic teachings.

View of the Shri Swaminarayan Hindu Mandir temple in northwest London. Often called the Neasden temple due to its location in a neighborhood of that name, this was the first Hindu temple built in England or Europe. The stone temple was designed and built according to ancient instructions in the Vedas, using no structural steel.

Hinduism also began to spread beyond the Indian subcontinent, as Indians living under British rule were encouraged to emigrate to other parts of the empire. In this way, Hindu communities sprang up on all the continents of the world. Whereas earlier, Hinduism had been entirely Indian, now it became a global religion.

Modern India and Its Neighbors

After the end of the Second World War, the European powers no longer had the military strength to hold onto their far-flung colonies. They began a process of granting the colonies their independence. The British decided to divide India into two separate independent countries in 1947. India would be primarily populated by Hindus, while Pakistan would be mostly Muslim. Unfortunately, this led to violence in both of the newly independent countries, as Muslims were forced to flee from India as refugees, while Hindus in Pakistan were similarly attacked by the Muslim majority.

In 1971 a third state came into existence when the region known as East Pakistan broke away from Pakistan to create the new state of Bangladesh. Like Pakistan, most people in Bangladesh are Muslims.

The State of India is constitutionally a secular nation, which means it has no state-sponsored religion. However, Hindus are a majority in India, and they often pressure the government to favor Hindu interests. This led to the formation of the Bharatiya Janata Party (BJP), meaning "the people's party of Hindu India." As of 2017, the BJP is the most powerful political party in India, as it is supported by most of the country's 965 million Hindus. The other major party is the Indian National Congress, which played an important role in the independence movement of the early twentieth century. This party tends to be favored by India's religious minorities, including its more than 170 million Muslims and nearly 21 million Sikhs. Members of these groups often feel underprivileged and threatened by the Hindu majority.

Since the 1947 partition, tensions between the Hindu and Muslim communities have surfaced and occasionally flared up. A new trend of Hinduism has arisen to counter the Christian and Muslim influences absorbed in India over the previous 500 years. The new fundamentalist kind of Hinduism resists the influences of western culture and western values in India.

Global Hinduism

Hinduism is also growing outside of India. The religion has become part of the fabric of many countries in the West, as Hindus have settled there and brought up successive generations in the Hindu tradition. As Hindu communities prosper in Europe and the United States, they have built more Hindu temples, and interest has grown in preserving and expressing Hindu culture. Contemporary Hinduism as an active religion in the West has been influenced by a number of international Hindu movements.

The Ramakrishna Mission was founded in Bengal in the nineteenth century by Vivekananda and named after his guru, Ramakrishna. In its monastic organization and its

Indian soldiers guard the border in the Kashmir region, an Indian province where many Muslims live. Pakistan and India have clashed several times over Kashmir since the countries became independent in 1947.

A Hare Krishna monk speaks to a group of Indian children in the state of Uttar Pradesh.

emphasis on welfare work through hospitals and schools, it was influenced by Christian missions in India. In the West, Ramakrishna Missions concentrate mainly on teaching meditation and Vedic philosophy.

The Swami Narayana Mission started in India, in Gujarat, early in the nineteenth century. It stressed devotion through education and community service, earning the respect of the British governors. Today it has a strong presence wherever Gujaratis have settled abroad, such as countries in Africa and the Americas, and in the UK. Its temples are often elaborate works of craftsmanship wrought from marble and stone. In the West, the Mission runs several Hindu schools.

The Visva Hindu Parisad, meaning "World Hindu Association," was formed in 1964 in reaction to the Indian government's secular policy, to promote traditional Hinduism in a non-sectarian way. The Association is dedicated to reawakening Hindu consciousness and fostering cooperation of Hindus throughout the world. Its emphasis is on a universal and inclusive form of Hinduism.

Another group that runs Hindu schools in the West is the Hare Krishna movement. It is based on devotion to Krishna as taught in the Bhagavad Gita. Although the roots of the movement are in Bengal, on the Indian subcontinent, a large proportion of its members are not of Indian origin, making it a truly international form of Hinduism.

 ## Text-Dependent Questions

1. What is the cycle of samsara?
2. What are the four castes of Hinduism? What are those who are not a member of one of these castes called?
3. What was the period of British rule over India called?

 ## Research Project

Using the Internet or your school library, research the story of one of Hinduism's many important deities. A few examples are Ganesha, Shiva, Krishna, Rama, Hanuman, Vishnu, Lakshmi, Rama, Durga, Kali, or Saraswati. Write a two-page report about the deity and present it to your class.

Hindu traditions are passed from one generation to another, at such meeting places as Varanasi, where the faithful gather to bathe in the Ganges River.

 ## Words to Understand in This Chapter

bhaktyi yoga—the path of devotional service to the eternal spiritual truth (Brahman). The word *bhakti* means "devotion."

brahmin—a teacher or priest in traditional Hindu society.

jnana yoga—the path of knowledge of the eternal spiritual truth (Brahman). The word *jnana* means "knowledge."

karma yoga—the path of dedicating actions to the Supreme, thus gaining freedom from the consequences of action.

Lakshmi—goddess of fortune, who accompanies Vishnu.

mantra—a spiritual sound vibration on which to focus the mind and the senses. From the Sanskrit words man ("mind") and tra ("release").

Tourists visit the famous Hindu temple in the Batu Caves of Kuala Lumpur, Malaysia.

3 How Hindus Live and Worship

Although some traditional patterns of Hindu family life are changing in the West, as more Hindus adopt western ways, certain parts of the Hindu tradition remain unaltered.

Hindus strive to be vegetarian, to make regular visits to the temple, to pray or meditate early in the morning, to keep a shrine in the home where food is regularly offered to God, and to decorate the home with pictures of Hindu deities. Many Hindus do not smoke or drink alcohol, but this varies between households, and even between members of a family.

The four basic aims of the Hindu way of life are religion (*dharma*), prosperity (*artha*), enjoyment (*kama*), and liberation (*moksha*).

Hindus believe that practicing the basics of their religion, such as being dutiful, truthful, and nonviolent, will bring the enjoyment of a happy home and life's basic comforts. Other pleasures, such as music, dance, good food, and festivals, are also all part of the Hindu way of life. Once someone has found worldly fulfilment through religion, prosperity, and enjoyment, that person will realize that the fundamental problems of life remain. They are birth, old age, disease, and death. Therefore the final and greatest goal of the Hindu way of life is liberation from the cycle of birth and death.

The Important Role of Gurus

The core of Hindu teachings is "disciplic succession." This means that the essence of the most important Hindu teachings are traditionally passed from one generation to another through a system of discipleship and obedience.

When a disciple has passed the tests set by the teacher, he or she can learn the secrets of the Vedic teaching—the wisdom descended from the Vedas—which is thus preserved for the next generation. Three of the important ancient teachers from whom many modern gurus (teachers) claim descent are Shankara (780–812 CE), Ramanuja (1017–1137), and Madhva (1238–1317).

This system of guru and disciple has kept Hinduism alive for thousands of years, without the need for a central hierarchy or single authority. Hinduism has very little formal structure outside the network of gurus, priests, and holy people and their *ashrams*. These are centers of learn-

Hindus attend the Mahashivatri Festival at the Pashupatinath Temple in Kathmandu, Nepal.

ing and spiritual practice, which are found at important holy places throughout India.

Well-established families have links to ancestral lineages of gurus, from whom they have received guidance and inspiration over many generations. Anyone wishing to be dedicated to spiritual practice will choose a guru as a personal teacher. The pupil will have to demonstrate his or her sincerity through respect and obedience to the guru, who in return will train that person in spiritual practice and in the scriptures.

Sages of the Mountain

Many holy people live as recluses in India. They are known as *sadhus*. They live in caves on mountain slopes in the Himalayas, or in the depths of the forests, or on the banks of rivers. There, they practice daily meditation and teach their disciples.

The history of Hinduism owes a great deal to these teachers. Their simple lifestyle and lack of material possessions earns them a special respect from Hindus, who understand that the highest goal of life is to be detached from material goods, and to transcend the attraction of physical comforts and pleasures. There are many stories about the power and authority of these teachers, who include Vyasadeva, author of the *Mahabharata*, and Valmiki, author of the *Ramayana*.

All authentic gurus must trace their authority from the Vedas through the line of teachers from which they are descended.

The Importance of Family

Hindus place great importance on the family and family tradition. This is reflected in the lives of the favorite Hindu deities, for instance Rama, who protected his wife Sita, and mother Yasoda, and her mischievous child Krishna.

The extended family remains an important part of Hindu society, even in communities that have lived in the West for several generations. Parents are given respect because they possess wisdom and experience. Small children are given lots of affection and freedom, and the whole family shares in their upbringing. Elderly parents often live with their married children and their grandchildren, with two or three young families living together under the same roof as their parents. The grandparents are regarded as the spiritual authorities and leaders in the community, giving stability and continuity to the tradition.

The Four Stages of Life

The journey of life is traditionally divided into four stages, called the "four ashrams." Each ashram lasts about 25 years.

Up to the age of 25 is the student stage, for studying the scriptures and learning the practice of yoga. It is called *brahmacharya*. Next comes household life, called *grihastha*. In this stage, a Hindu is encouraged to be active in the

A fisherman works with his children preparing their fishing nets in Goa, India. They belong to a community of fishermen, and their sons are destined to be fishermen like them. Such social restrictions limit personal freedom, but Hindus believe that they also ensure the stability of society.

world, to earn money, to raise a family, and to be involved in supporting the community. Around the age of 50 comes retired life, called *vanaprastha*, when the children are grown up and can support themselves. At this stage in life, a Hindu is encouraged to practice austerity, to go on pilgrimage, and to be dedicated to the service of others. The final stage, reserved only for a few, is when a person gives up all worldly possessions and all ties to the family and society. This is called *sannyasi* and is the sacred order most respected by Hindus.

The Four Varnas

In traditional Hindu society everyone had a duty based on that person's abilities and nature. There were four main divisions of society, or varnas, which corresponded to the head, the arms, the torso, and the legs. The head (*brahmin*) was associated with teaching and intellectual work; the arms (*kshatriya*) with administration, politics, law, and order; the torso (*vaishya*) with commerce, trade, and farming; the legs (*sudra*) with arts and crafts, skilled trades, and manual labor.

Each of these parts of society, like the parts of the body, has a different but equally important role to play. Today this system is not so strictly applied.

This is partly because it deteriorated into a rigid caste system, which created a very unequal society. But the concept of social duty is still influential among Hindus. An important feature of the system is that spiritual and political leadership are separate.

How Hindus Worship

The Hindu tradition has always emphasized that God is everywhere, even in your own heart. Therefore worship is not confined to a temple building.

There are four main places where Hindus practice their worship. The first place is the temple of the heart and mind. The body is a temple of God, and the form of God remembered in the mind is sacred. Second is the household shrine, which is found in most Hindu homes. The third is the public temple—every Hindu community has at least one. The fourth is on a pilgrimage. It is common practice for Hindus to go on pilgrimages to famous holy places, sometimes traveling great distances.

A Hindu temple is the home of God. At the heart of the temple is a small shrine room that houses the murti of a deity, such as Vishnu, Devi, or Shiva. There may also be secondary shrines dedicated to other deities in the temple.

The main deity lives in the central part of the temple and is served by priests. In the early hours of the morning the priests "wake up" the deity, bathing and clothing it. At intervals during the day the priests perform the ceremony of arati, when they light a lamp and offer it to the deity before passing it among worshippers as a blessing. The priests also make regular offerings of food to be blessed and distributed to worshippers. In front of the deity room is the hall where worshippers gather to sing prayers or hear the teachings of the scriptures. At night, the deity "sleeps" and the temple is closed.

Hindu Worship at Home

Most Hindu families keep a household shrine dedicated to their own deities. Often the shrine also includes pictures of their guru and their deceased relatives. Worship in the home is part of the daily rhythm of life. Food cooked in the kitchen is first offered to the deity along with flowers and incense to sanctify the home.

Hindus worship at a shrine in the Shiva temple of Munneswaram, Sri Lanka. The shrine is decorated with ornate reliefs and colorful patterns.

It is quite common for the elders of the family such as the grandparents, to maintain a regular and devout cycle of daily worship. On festival days and special family occasions, the shrine becomes the focus for the whole family.

Meditation and Yoga

The main methods of spiritual practice in Hinduism are the different forms of yoga. The literal meaning of *yoga* is "link," referring to union with God. Yoga offers a path of discipline leading to God, and can be a whole way of life.

The most popular forms of yoga practiced by Hindus are karma yoga and bhakti yoga. *Karma yoga* is the path of selfless service, either to other people or to God. *Bhakti*

An Indian man stands in Vrikshasana ("Tree Pose"). Certain elements of jnana yoga have become popular in Western cultures as exercise.

yoga is the path of devotion to God through prayer, worship, and service. Central to bhakti yoga is the chanting of a mantra as a regular offering of devotion.

Another yoga path is *jnana yoga*, which is the yoga of knowledge through discrimination and study of the scriptures. Raja yoga, or royal yoga, is the form of yoga popularly practiced in the West, though not usually in its complete eightfold form.

The sage Patanjali, who lived in the third century CE, divided the path of yoga into eight aspects, or "limbs." To practice yoga properly, means learning to integrate each of the eight aspects into your life. These are:

- *yama*—moral and ethical code of practice, such as nonviolence and truthfulness
- *niyama*—personal discipline, such as cleanliness and self-control
- *asana*—posture and sitting, so as to be alert, relaxed, and peaceful. This is also known as *hatha yoga,* and is widely practiced in the West)
- *pranayama*—breath control as an aid to finding stillness and peace in the mind
- *pratyahara*—withdrawing the mind from the senses so as to concentrate inward
- *dharana*—concentrating the mind to be one-pointed, without any distractions
- *dhyana*—meditation, the complete form of inner concentration of the self
- *samadhi*—super-consciousness, or union with God.

Hindu Rites of Passage

The journey of the soul through life, from conception to the final departure, is marked with ceremonies called *samskaras*. These remind Hindus of the sanctity of life and invoke divine blessings at each stage. Nowadays, only some are the ceremonies are performed.

On either the tenth or the twelfth day following a child's birth, the name-giving ceremony takes place. At the same time, the child is taken outside the house and shown the sun for the first time, symbolizing the journey from the dark world of non-being to the world of light and being.

A couple prepare to exchange their vows at a Hindu wedding ceremony. They pray to live a long life together in health and happiness.

At five months old, the child is fed grains for the first time, and when the child is either one, three, or five years old, the child's head is shaved as a symbol of purity.

Hindu marriage brings prosperity and good fortune. It is the cornerstone of community life. Many Hindu parents choose a partner for their son or daughter by arrangement with another family. If either partner does not wish to marry the person chosen, he or she has the right to refuse.

Traditionally, a husband's duty is to protect his wife, and hers is to serve her husband. At a deeper level, the marriage is a partnership of two souls who help each other to grow in love and understanding of God.

At the wedding ceremony, the couple exchange vows in front of a sacred fire. The bride says: "May my husband have a long life. May my family prosper. Let this fire make me and my husband one."

Then the bridegroom says: "Let your glory increase day by day. Let us be in good health. Let us together lead a harmonious life for a hundred years." Together they then walk around the sacrificial fire and, as they take seven steps, the bride prays to Vishnu.

At death, when the soul is about to leave the body, a few drops of water (ideally from the Ganges River) and leaves of the sacred tulasi plant, are placed in the mouth. After death, the body is washed and dressed in new cloth, then carried in procession to the cremation ground, where verses from the Bhagavad Gita are recited for the peace of the soul. After cremation, the flowers, bones, and ashes are scattered in the nearest sacred river, or in the ocean.

Hindu women chant in a temple in Vrindava.

Sacred Places

Hindus establish new sacred places wherever they go in the world. But they have special reverence for the Indian sub-continent, the birthplace of Hindu traditions. The rivers, mountains, and forests of India figure in Hinduism's sacred stories, including the descent from heaven of the River Ganges, the exile of Rama to the Dandakaranya forest, Krishna's bathing in the Yamuna River at Vrindavan, and

Sadhus and pilgrims on the streets near the temple of Badrinatha, northern India.

his construction of a great sea-fort in Dwaraka Bay. The subcontinent is full of sacred places associated with different incarnations of God and holy teachers.

The Hindu word for a sacred place is *tirtha*. It means "crossing-place"—the place where the soul can pass from this world to the next. The four holy places of India are Badrinatha, in the north; Puri, in the east; Ramesvaram, in the south; and Dvaraka, in the west. Many Hindus make a vow to visit all of these in their lifetime. Three other ancient holy towns are Ayodhya, the birthplace of Rama; Mathura, the birthplace of Krishna; and Varanasi, which is sacred to Shiva.

The River Ganges and her tributary, the Yamuna, are sacred to Vishnu, Shiva, and Krishna. They rise in the Himalayas and flow into the Bay of Bengal. The River Sindhu, or Indus, flows from the Himalayas across Pakistan to the Arabian Sea. Three other great, sacred rivers—the Narmada, Godavari, and Kaveri—rise in southern India. The seventh sacred river is the mythical river Sarasvati, which is believed to flow underground across northern India.

Hindu Pilgrimages

The desire to travel is a natural human urge. Historically, people of all cultures went on pilgrimages to great, sacred places. In this way, they saw the world. Only in the modern age has pilgrimage been replaced by tourism.

In India, pilgrimage is still the principal reason for travel. Every year, hundreds of millions of Hindu pilgrims trav-

Hindu pilgrims bathe in the Ganges River at Har Ki Pauri, a famous landmark in Haridwar, India. This revered place is the site of the Kumbha Mela pilgrimage every twelve years, most recently in 2016.

el across the length and breadth of the Indian subcontinent (which includes India, Pakistan, Bangladesh, Bhutan, and Nepal). They go to keep a vow, to fix the mind on God, to meet holy teachers, to seek companionship, and to find inspiration.

The pilgrimage of Kumbha Mela attracts more than 120 million pilgrims, making it the biggest religious gathering the world has ever seen. The pilgrimage is held at four sites, which rotate about every three years, meaning each of these sacred sites hosts a pilgrimage every twelve years. The sites are all located in the modern nation of India. They include the ancient city of Haridwar, on the banks of the Ganges River; Prayag (Allahabad), where the Ganges and Yamuna rivers converge; Ujjain, on the Shipra River; and Nasik, on the Godavari River.

The Hindu Calendar

Hindus calculate important dates and religious festivals according to a lunar calendar, that follows the cycles of the moon. The 12 Hindu months are Magha, Phalguna, Chaitra, Vaisakha, Jaistha, Asadha, Shravanah, Bhandra, Aswin, Kartika, Agrahayana, Paus. Each month begins on the day after the full moon or, in southern India, with the new moon. Each month lasts 30 days, so the Hindu year is several days shorter than the solar year, which western calendars follow. To even this out, every few years an extra lunar month, called Adhik, is added to the Hindu calendar.

Hindu festivals are occasions for coming together, for storytelling, for praying, for singing, and for fasting or feasting. Some festivals coincide with the full moon or the new moon. The 15 days of the waxing moon are called the "bright days," and those of the waning moon are the "dark days."

The spring festival, called Holi, takes place on the full-moon day, or 15th bright day, of the lunar month Phalguna. This usually falls in March.

Holi is an occasion of merriment, high spirits, and bonfires. People go on to the streets and throw colored water and powders to recall Krishna's childhood play and welcome the coming of spring.

Krishna's birthday is celebrated at the festival of Janmastami, which usually falls in August. Krishna was born at midnight in a prison house. Devotees fast all day, and in the evening sing songs as they rock a cradle with an image of the child Krishna inside. At midnight they break their fast by feasting.

Diwali, the Festival of Lights, usually takes place in October. The festival honors *Lakshmi*, goddess of wealth, and celebrates the triumph of light over darkness, or good over evil. On the darkest day of the month of Kartika, lamps decorate houses to welcome back the hero Rama and his wife, Sita, from exile in the forest. Their return is joyously celebrated with fireworks. For many Hindus, the following day is the start of the new year. The festival of Diwali is also celebrated by followers of the Sikh faith.

 Text-Dependent Questions

1. What are the eight aspects of yoga?
2. What seven rivers do Hindus consider sacred?

 Research Project

Using your school library or the internet, find out more about one of the Hindu festivals mentioned in this chapter, such as Holi, Janmastami, or Diwali. Present your findings to the class in a two-page report.

 ## Words to Understand in This Chapter

Ayurveda—the traditional Hindu system of medicine, which is based on the idea of balance in bodily systems and uses diet, herbal treatment, and yogic breathing.

incarnate—to be embodied in flesh, especially a deity in human form.

multicultural—constituting several cultural or ethnic groups within a society.

A Hindu shrine to Brahma, the four-faced creator god, in Las Vegas. Most Hindus in the United States are immigrants from South Asia or their descendants.

4 Hinduism's Influence on the West

hindu culture, with its vibrant temples, arts, fashions, and food, has brought much that is new and valuable to *multicultural* societies in the West. Hinduism's informality, and the open-mindedness shown toward different religious traditions, appeals to westerners looking for greater freedom of religious expression. Hindu practices such as yoga, meditation, astrology, alternative medicines, and vegetarian health diets have attracted widespread interest.

Karma, reincarnation, and other Hindu ideas are becoming widely absorbed among the informal beliefs of many people. Karma encourages us to take responsibility for our behavior and to learn from our mistakes. In today's world, when human actions affect the global environment so profoundly, "karmic" consequences are increasingly of concern to us all. Modern society encourages individual freedom, so the idea of taking responsibility for one's own actions is an important concept.

Yoga and Meditation

Yoga, with its emphasis on personal transformation, offers people a proven way of enhancing their own lives through exercises and routines that anyone can learn and practice. There are many organizations, originating within Hinduism and now extending beyond its traditional bound-

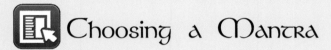 Choosing a Mantra

A mantra is an aid to meditation. It generally consists of a word or sound that is repeated numerous times, allowing the person to clear their mind and focus their thoughts.

The Sanskrit word *Om* (pronounced A-U-M-mmmm) is commonly used as a mantra to prepare a believer for silent meditation. Hindus consider this to be a sacred sound and a spiritual icon (depicted at right). Another well-known Hindu mantra is the following phrase:

"Hare Krishna, Hare Krishna, Krishna Krishna, Hare Hare.
"Hare Rama, Hare Rama, Rama Rama, Hare Hare"

This mantra is often repeated softly as a devotional prayer.

How to Meditate

Try sitting quietly for 20 minutes in a peaceful setting. Sit on a cushion on the floor, with your legs crossed, or on a chair with your back straight. Begin by concentrating on your breathing, making it deep and regular, and relaxing your body and mind. After a while your mind will calm down and naturally become focused. Then concentrate your mind on the region of your heart and begin to repeat your mantra, either in a soft voice or silently in your mind. If you do this every day, gradually increasing length of meditation time to an hour or more, Hindus believe you will soon notice a difference in your life.

aries, that offer guidance and tuition in meditation and yoga.

Transcendental meditation (TM), is practiced by some 5 million people worldwide. It became famous when, in 1965, the popular music group the Beatles travelled to India to meet its founder, Maharishi Mahesh Yogi. While there, they stayed at his ashram in the Himalayas.

Partly as a result of the Beatles' great popularity, TM rapidly spread across continents. Today, TM remains particularly popular in the United Kingdom. Broadcasts go out every day of the week via a network of eight satellite channels. The broadcasts include education programs to teach science, technology, and healthcare according to the principles laid down in the Vedas.

Hindu Vegetarianism

Hinduism teaches that all creatures are God's children. All life is sacred because the soul can be *incarnated* into any life form, so animals should be treated with care and respect. There are karmic consequences for inflicting suffering on other beings. We should treat all creatures— human or animal—as we would wish to be treated ourselves, Hindus say. For these reasons, a high proportion of Hindus are vegetarian.

The yoga tradition stresses the importance of a healthy diet. It divides foods into three kinds: those that give vitality, those that create disease, and those that cause tiredness. The human digestive system, it says, functions better on a balanced vegetarian diet. Compared to meat and fish, vegetarian foods tend to be low in fat and high in fiber.

Vegetarian food is also safer, because it contains much lower levels of chemical additives than does meat.

As well as being healthy, vegetarian cooking can also be very tasty. There are many good vegetarian cookery books on the market, with lots of delicious recipes to try.

Hindu tradition is against eating animals, not only because it is considered cruel and unnecessary, but because it is wasteful of the earth's resources. Fattening animals for

Cows stroll through the city of Pushkar, India. Most Hindus respect the cow for its gentle nature, which they feel represents the main teaching of Hinduism.

slaughter uses up valuable grains that could be fed directly to people, especially in poorer countries. The big herds of animals favored by modern farming also require the large-scale clearance of land, a heavier use of chemicals, and the production of more polluting substances. All this is against the Hindu tradition of small-scale, humane farming.

A vegetarian diet, according to yoga philosophy, adapts the mind to more subtle and sensitive vibrations. This, in turn, produces greater spiritual awareness. The violence involved in a meat diet, and the karma that this creates,

A Hindu man prepares a traditional vegetarian meal. Before it is eaten, the food will be blessed with prayers as a reminder that all food is a gift of God.

coarsens both the mind and the senses, making it more difficult to attain spiritual awareness.

Hindu Medicine

Hinduism has its own complete system of medicine. It is called *Ayurveda* and is thousands of years old. Ayurveda recognizes three basic "humors" that regulate the body and mind. They are known by the Sanskrit names *vata* (wind), *pitta* (bile) and *kapha* (mucus). They correspond to the elements: vata is a combination of air and the ether; pitta is a combination of fire and water; kapha is a combination of water and earth. When these three humors are in balance, the body is healthy, but when one or another of them is in excess, this causes disease.

Educational Video

To watch a brief introduction to Ayurvedia, scan here

Each of us has a constitution that belongs to one of these three types, Hindus say. The balance of our health can be maintained by eating and living in accordance with our individual type. Ayurvedic treatment is based on the use of herbs and diet to correct any imbalance in a person's constitution.

Ayurveda is gaining ground in the West as part of the trend toward alternative medicine and a move away from the powerful drugs prescribed by modern medicine. Drugs can often create imbalances in the body, not cure them.

The essential characteristic of Ayurveda, which makes it different from ordinary, conventional Western medicine, is that it stresses prevention as the key to good health. By living and eating in a healthy way, and with regular exercise and good habits, you have a better chance of not falling ill.

Ill health, says Ayurveda, has three main causes: negative emotions, for instance anger or fear; eating too much food, or eating the wrong kind of food for one's constitution; and lack of personal hygiene. Ayurvedic cures are based on herbal remedies, massage, and cleansing diets, as

Mohandas K. Gandhi (1869–1948) became a hero to many people around the world because of his successful use of nonviolence in gaining Indian independence from Great Britain. Among those that Gandhi inspired was the Rev. Martin Luther King Jr., who adapted Gandhi's nonviolent tactics for the African-American Civil Rights Movement during the 1950s and 1960s.

well as changes in lifestyle, yoga, and meditation to calm the mind.

Health farms, which are popular in the West, are a largely Hindu invention, originating in traditional yoga cures. On a health farm, patients follow special diets with a routine of exercises and massage in a stress-free environment. In India, many middle-class Hindus visit special yoga clinics, where they are restored to good health by cleansing their bodies and minds through yoga diets and exercises.

The Principle of Nonviolence

Nonviolence, called *ahimsa*, is an important part of Hindu tradition. It has been emphasized particularly by the Jain religion, which is a distinct faith of its own but is related to Hindu tradition. The principle behind nonviolence is that, according to the law of *karma*, any harm that a person does to another creature will come back to that person in the future. That belief explains why many Hindus do not eat meat and are vegetarian.

A famous champion of *ahimsa* was Mohandas K. Gandhi. Known as Mahatma Gandhi, he was an Indian politician and nationalist leader in the 1940s during India's struggle for independence from British rule. Gandhi refused to use violence against the British. Instead, he and his followers used nonviolent, passive resistance, such as gathering together and refusing to disperse when ordered to do so. Gandhi was arrested many times, but his methods hastened the departure of the British, who left India in 1947, paving the way for Indian independence.

 ## Text-Dependent Questions

1. What music group helped make Transcendental Meditation popular in the 1960s?
2. Why do many Hindus follow a vegetarian diet?

 ## Research Project

Using your school library or the internet, research the question, "Should you give to charity?" One perspective is that the world is unfair—the three wealthiest people in the world have more money than the 48 poorest countries combined, and millions of children die each year from poverty-related illnesses. So those who have more than they need should help those who lack enough resources to meet even basic needs. On the other hand, people deserve the money they have earned and should be able to spend it as they wish. Some people feel that charity demeans people and makes them dependent on others. Present your conclusion in a two-page report, providing examples from your research that support your answer.

 Words to Understand in This Chapter

euthanasia—the painless killing of a patient who is suffering from an incurable disease or in an irreversible coma. The practice is illegal in most countries.

sadhu—saintly person.

sari—a silk or cotton wrap-around dress worn by Hindu women.

A Hindu farm family plants cabbage in a field near the village of Amravati. The traditional simple way of life is highly valued in India, but it is also changing fast.

5 Challenges that Hindus Face Today

T raditionally, the Hindu way of life has been based on the extended family. Today, in the West, that pattern may be changing along with other traditions. In western countries, young Hindus who go off to college mingle in an environment quite unlike the one they have been used to, where people live their lives differently. After completing their college studies, many young Hindus never move back into the family home. They start a new way of life modeled on the society around them. Others, who seek to retain their Hindu cultural roots, find new ways of expressing them. As a result, new forms of Hinduism are emerging in Europe and North America.

It is normal for there to be tensions between generations. But these are magnified when children grow up in an altogether different society from the one that nurtured their parents and grandparents. This is the case with the second and third generation of Hindu immigrant families in the West. Even Hindu marriage is changing, with divorce, which in traditional Hindu society is almost non-existent, becoming more accepted among Hindus in western countries. Yet, despite outside cultural and social pressures, the Hindu tradition of obedience to the authority of parents remains strong.

A key to cultural continuity is language. Most Hindu families living in the West have kept their mother tongue, which preserves many of their religious and cultural traditions. That language may be Gujarati, Punjabi, Hindi, Bengali, or one of the many other languages native to India. Efforts are made to pass on the language to younger generations by means of special classes held in temples and community centers. But despite this, outside India traditional languages are gradually falling out of use.

Another tradition is the *sari*, a long, silk or cotton wraparound dress, worn by Hindu women in India. In the West the *sari* is becoming less common among Hindu women, as they conform more to western fashions. But many will still put on a *sari* to visit a temple, for festival celebrations, or to attend a social occasion such as a wedding.

The Best of Both Worlds

Research has shown that children growing up in Hindu families, but within the host culture of a western country, are often well equipped to take advantage of the best of both worlds. This helps them find stability in their lives. That is

When Indian families move to western countries like Great Britain or the United States, the younger generations often embrace western culture, while also trying to maintain their traditional religious and cultural practices

why Hindu family traditions can be expected to remain strong and healthy, even though family behavior may change in response to new social patterns.

Many Hindus living in the United States, Great Britain, or other western nations have family and community ties back in India. As these Hindu immigrants prosper they are often able to help their ancestral communities by providing financial or social support. A challenge for the future will be to maintain and strengthen these ties, which are beneficial to both Hindu communities and to the world at large.

Some Hindus growing up in the West feel uncertain of where they fit in. This is especially true of those from religious homes, where more liberal moral and social habits are frowned upon. Often there is a lack of understanding about Hinduism in society, even among some young Hindus. Although they may visit Hindu temples and join in with their festivals, many of them lose touch with basic Hindu beliefs and teachings. But others are showing signs of a desire to explore their cultural roots and learn more about their faith.

When Hindus first settled in the West, they lived mostly in inner-city areas, where they met with prejudice. But as

Statue of Ganesha, an elephant-headed deity. Hindus consider Ganesha to be the lord of success and a patron deity of arts and sciences.

they became more established in the wider community, the prejudice diminished. Today they are part of mainstream western society and are active in all walks of life. Within the Hindu community itself there is sometimes prejudice between different social groups. Some tightly knit immigrant communities still resist intermarrying, or even mixing socially, with people of other faiths.

Among Hindus, there is less resistance to mixed marriages than there used to be. For the younger Hindu generation in Europe and North America, these are liberating and exciting times. Young Hindus are mixing more outside their own community and defining new identities for themselves as western Hindus.

Arjuna is one of the key figures in the ancient Sanskrit epic Mahabharata. He was considered to be a great warrior and archer. Arjuna also plays an important role in the Bhagavad Gita, alongside Krishna.

Hindu Teachings in the Modern World

In Western society, success is measured in terms of possessions, while people follow a lifestyle that consumes more than the earth can afford. This has been called "high living and simple thinking." By contrast, Hinduism teaches the value of a simple life. Living simply, Hindus say, keeps us closer to nature and to God, bringing more happiness. All the world's religions agree that the highest standard of life is the simplest. This is known as "simple living and high thinking."

Vandana Shiva, an Indian scientist and environmental activist, says three Hindu teachings stand out in today's world:

1 All people of different faiths are your brothers and sisters.
2 Do not take more than you need. As Mahatma Gandhi said, "The earth has enough for everyone's need, but not for everyone's greed."
3 We all have the capacity to take responsibility for our own lives and to be teachers and leaders by our personal example.

How Do Hindus Care for the Environment?

Hindus revere rivers, mountains, forests, and animals as sacred, and love to be close to nature. Many Hindu villages have a sacred lake, surrounded by a grove of trees to catch rainfall and protect the banks of the lake from erosion. Together the lake and the trees store water for irrigating the fields and supplying the wells in the village with drinking water. Not only are such landscapes serene, but they also serve as habitats for wildlife.

Unfortunately, in recent times these simple techniques for gathering and protecting clean water have been neglected. This has led to serious water shortages and, in many parts of India, to the spread of desert land. Hindu practices of caring for nature are being forgotten, making human survival in this environment more difficult.

Indian scientist Vandana Shiva is an important environmental activist. She is motivated by her Hindu beliefs to stand up for the rights of rural women and farmers. She fought against the sale of genetically modified "terminator" seeds in India, because they produce only one crop. This means farmers have to buy new seeds each year from the suppliers.

Environmental activist Vandana Shiva has written more than twenty books, most of which encourage the continuation of traditional Hindu practices.

She has also campaigned against companies trying to patent the sacred Neem tree. Hindu stories tell of how this tree came from a drop of divine nectar carried to earth. Neem provides a natural and harmless alternative to pesticides, but multinational business corporations have tried to patent it for their own use.

Hinduism, Drugs, and Sex

Usually, among Hindus, it is only the men who drink alcohol. But habits vary from one community to another, depending on factors such as caste and cultural background. Drugs are generally regarded as harmful to mental and physical well-being. In India, some *sadhus* who worship Shiva smoke cannabis, but this tradition has not made the habit acceptable to the general Hindu community.

In the Hindu tradition, sexual restraint is valued as promoting health and a long life. Sex outside marriage is

Jagat Prakash Nadda, the Minister for Health and Family Welfare of India, speaks to the United Nations General Assembly about the problem of HIV/AIDS infection.

strongly discouraged, and sexuality in any form is rarely discussed among Hindus, in India and elsewhere.

The sacred Hindu texts do not universally condemn homosexuality, and some of them include stories with homosexual characters and themes. However, most older Hindus refuse to talk about or even to acknowledge homo-sexuality, although this tendency is beginning to change among younger Indian Hindus.

For these reasons, education about HIV/AIDS and safe sex practices face obstacles in traditional Hindu society. As a consequence, India faced a serious AIDS epidemic in the late 1990s and early 2000. However, better education in recent years has led to an overall reduction in new HIV infections.

Hindu Views About the Elderly

The overall attitude of Hinduism toward life and death is one of acceptance rather than struggle. Old age and the gradual decline of the body as death draws nearer are not necessarily seen as being bad. Old age brings wisdom and the opportunity to devote more time to prayer and spiritual practice. In Hindu society elderly people command an authority and respect that provides an important anchor for the community. They are treated by everyone with a great deal of affection.

For Hindus, there is no taboo connected with death. When death comes, it is allowed to happen as a part of the inevitable cycle of reincarnation.

When someone dies, their remains are cremated as soon

A funeral pyre in the Bagmati river in Kathmandu, Nepal. Traditionally, all adult Hindus are cremated. The cremation ceremony includes a number of specific rituals.

as possible, to help the soul let go of the dead body and continue on the journey of reincarnation and spiritual growth.

Traditionally, Hinduism is opposed to suicide, although sometimes people did deliberately end their lives by fasting in a holy place. In the debate over *euthanasia*, or mercy killing, Hindus believe that nature should take its natural course, without interference either to prolong life or to hasten its end.

Hinduism and Women's Rights

Today, it is not unusual for women to be major Hindu religious leaders. For much of the twentieth century, Anandamayi had a large following throughout India. More recently, teachers such as Mother Gayathri, in Britain, and Nirmila Devi, in the United States, have risen to prominence. One of India's most famous politicians was also a woman. Indira Gandhi was twice India's prime minister, but was assassinated in 1984, during her second term.

In the Indian towns of Barsana and Nandgaon, in the state of Uttar Pradesh, a festival known as Lath mar Holi is celebrated a few days before the traditional Hindu festival of Holi. As part of the festival, Hindu women beat up men with long sticks, recreating a legend about Krishna's ancient visit to Barsana.

This has not always been the case, however, as historically Hindu social customs often put women at a disadvantage compared to men. These customs included child-marriages, in which young girls were betrothed to much older men; the practice of *sati*, in which a Hindu widow was expected to join her dead husband on his funeral pyre and burn to death (though this seldom happened); polygamy, which allowed a man to have two or more wives; and the dowry system, which required a young woman to bring a substantial gift of money or land to her future husband.

Today, in India, women's rights are an important issue and many of the old, unfair practices are being swept away. However, as in most parts of the world, men remain dominant in public life.

What the Future Holds

Hinduism is a very ancient religion, with a philosophy that dates back at least 3,500 years, and possibly much longer. It has stood the test of time. Although the world changes, and people's lives change, the essential teachings of Hinduism will remain much the same as they have always been. That is Hinduism's strength. Its fundamental truths have been relevant to generations down the ages and still are today.

Future generations will see a significant change in Hinduism. From being a religion confined to a particular race of people and a particular land, it is shifting across the globe to become a religion that belongs to peoples of all races and all lands. This change is bound to produce a flowering of new ideas and new ways of expressing Hinduism's ancient truths.

It has been said that the twenty-first century will belong to India and China, the two most populous nations on earth. Unlike China, India is a democracy, meaning that the people elect the country's leaders. In terms of population,

Hare Krishnas pass out literature at a religious festival in Montreal, Canada. Hinduism is spreading throughout the world in the twenty-first century.

Educational Video

To see an example of traditional Hindu dance, scan here:

which is still expanding, India is the world's largest democracy. But India's economy lags behind those of the United States, China, Japan, and the major countries of the European Union, such as Germany, France, and the United Kingdom. For India to sustain its economic growth and provide for its vast population, its leaders will have to find a way to balance Hinduism's ecological traditions with modern ways of exploiting the country's natural resources.

Much of the environmental crisis facing the planet today is due to the way that people in the West live their lives and use up valuable resources. We may all need the softer influence of eastern faiths and cultures, such as Hinduism, to restore the delicate balance between nature and the way that is used to serve human needs.

As Hindu families settle in the West, they establish their own social and community networks. Their children put down roots in their adopted countries, and become part of mainstream society. Many of the younger generation are going into commerce and business, or are being drawn into caring professions and becoming doctors, teachers, and social workers. Others prefer working in the arts or the media, and some are entering the world of politics and government.

They bring to their professions a subtly different approach to life to that of their colleagues. Through them, Hindu worldviews are entering mainstream society in Britain, North America, and Europe. As they prosper and become more successful, their influence will grow. In the future, Hindu ideas of spiritual equality, of nonviolence, and of the virtue of simplicity will become more accepted and shared by more people.

 Text-Dependent Questions

1. What is a critical key to cultural continuity?
2. How do Hindus feel about mixed marriages?
3. What is the view of most Hindus toward homosexuality?
4. What are some traditional Indian customs that put women at a disadvantage to men?

 Research Project

Using the Internet or your school library, do some research to answer the question "Should Hindu values apply to helping the planet?" Those who agree will say that every single person who acts with conviction can make a difference. Those who disagree with this perspective believe that the problems are too great for anyone acting alone to be able to make any difference. We are powerless to change the way the world is, they would likely argue. Present your conclusion in a two-page report, providing examples from your research that support your answer.

Religious Demographics

U.S. & Canada about 5.6 million people

Canada about 25 million people

U.S. about 225 million people

U.S. about 0.575 million

North and South America about 10 million people

Latin America about 543 million people

Europe about 2.1 million people

Europe about 0.5 million people

Europe about 550 million people

Europe about 50 million people

Israel 5.6 million people

Africa about 518 million people

Africa about 475 million people

Asia about 1179 million people

Asia about 350 million people

Asia about 550 million people

India about 18 million people

Asia about 950 million people

Australia and Oceania about 24 million people

Australia and Oceania about 0.7 million people

Christians
about 2.2 billion people

Muslims
about 1.6 billion people

Sikh
about 23 million people

Hindus
about 1 billion people

Jews
about 14 million people

Buddhist
about 576 million people

Christian	Islam	No religion	Hindu	Buddhist	Sikhism	Judaism	Others
31.5%	22.3%	15.4%	14.0%	5.3%	0.3%	0.2%	11%

Hinduism

Founded
Developed gradually in prehistoric times

Number of followers
Around 1 billion

Holy Places
River Ganges, especially at Varanasi (Benares). Several other places in India

Holy Books
Vedas, Upanishads, Mahabharata, Rarnayana

Holy Symbol
Aum

Buddhism

Founded
535 BCE in Northern India

Number of followers
Around 576 million

Holy Places
Bodh Gaya, Sarnath, both in northern India

Holy Books
Tripitaka

Holy Symbol
Eight-spoked wheel

Sikhism

Founded
Northwest India, 15th century CE

Number of followers
Around 23 million

Holy Places
There are five important, takhts, or seats of high authority: in Amritsar, Patna Sahib, Anandpur Sahib, Nanded, and Talwandi

Holy Books
The Guru Granth Sahib

Holy Symbol
The Khanda, the symbol of the Khalsa

Christianity

Founded
Around 30 CE, Jerusalem

Number of followers
Around 2.2 billion

Holy Places
Jerusalem and other sites
associated with the life of Jesus

Holy Books
The Bible
(Old and New Testament)

Holy Symbol
Cross

Judaism

Founded
In what is now Israel, around 2,000 BCE

Number of followers
Around 14 million

Holy Places
Jerusalem, especially
the Western Wall

Holy Books
The Torah

Holy Symbol
Seven-branched menorah (candle stand)

Islam

Founded
610 CE on the Arabian Peninsula

Number of followers
Around 1.6 billion

Holy Places
Makkah and Madinah, in Saudi Arabia

Holy Books   **Holy Symbol**
The Qur'an   Crescent and star

Quick Reference: Hinduism

Worldwide distribution

The number of Hindus is estimated at more than 1 billion, or approximately 15 percent of the world's population. About 95 percent of the world's Hindus live in India.

Historically, Indian civilizations had trade links throughout southeast Asia, and so Hinduism spread to many neighboring countries. These include Nepal and the modern-day states of Bangladesh and Pakistan, which historically were considered part of India. Hindu traders also brought their religion to places like Burma, Malaysia, and Indonesia. Although Indonesia is the world's most populous Muslim country, the island of Bali is 84 percent Hindu.

For many centuries India was part of the British Empire, and Hindus established communities in the United Kingdom and Canada, as well as in numerous British colonies of the nineteenth and early twentieth centuries: Mauritius, British Guiana (now the independent country of Guyana), Suriname, Trinidad and other Caribbean islands, and South Africa.

The United States is home to about 2.3 million Hindus. Most Hindu immigrants have come to the U.S. since 1980. Today, India is the second-largest source of immigrants to the United States annually, after Mexico.

Holy Places

Hindus consider many places to be sacred, including Badrinatha, in the north; Puri, in the east; Ramesvaram, in the south; and Dvaraka, in the west. Many Hindus make pilgrimages to each of these cities, as well as three other ancient holy places: Ayodhya, the birthplace of Rama; Mathura, the birthplace of Krishna; and Varanasi, which is sacred to Shiva.

Hindus hold seven rivers to be sacred. These include the Ganges and its tributary, the Yamuna; the Sindhu (or Indus) River; the Narmada; the Godavari ; the Kaveri; and they mythical Sarasvati River.

Festivals

The Hindu calendar is lunar, but extra months are added according to a regular schedule so that festivals always fall in the proper season each year. Each month lasts 30 days, divided into 15 days of the waxing moon (the "bright days") and 15 days of the waning moon (the "dark days").

Major Hindu festivals include Mahashivaratri (Shiva's birthday)on the 14th dark day of Magha; Holi (Spring festival), on the 15th bright day of Phalguna; Rama Navami (Rama's birthday) on the 9th bright day of Chaitra; Hanuman Jayanti (birthday of the monkey-god Hanuman) on the 15th bright day of Chaitra; Ratha Yatra (the Chariot festival), on the 2nd bright day of Asadha; Raksha Bandhana on the 15th bright day of Shravanah; Janmastami (Krishna's birthday) on the 8th dark day of Bhandra; and Diwali, the "Festival of Lights," on the 15th dark day of Kartika.

Oil lamps in a Hindu temple.

Hinduism Timeline

3000 bce	According to ancient traditions, Krishna speaks the Bhagavad.
2000 bce	The first Vedic hymns are recorded in Sanskrit.
ca. 200 ce	Patanjali writes his Yoga-sutras, dividing the path of yoga into eight aspects.
780-812	Shankara founds Advaita, the impersonal school of Hinduism.
1017-1137	Ramanuja establishes the Vaishnava devotional tradition in South India.
1020	Islamic forces enter India under Mahmud of Ghazni.
1370-1440	Ramananda, with his follower Kabir, combines Hindu and Muslim teachings.
1469-1539	Nanak, influenced by Kabir, founds the Sikh religion in the Punjab region.
1486-1533	Caitanya, teaches the Vaishnava devotional movement in North India.
1785	Bhagavad Gita first translated into English, by Charles Wilkins.
1869	Mohandas K. Gandhi is born. He would lead India to independence.

late 1800s	Hindus begin to settle in countries of the British Empire after India becomes an official possession.
1893	Vivekananda represents Hinduism at the World Parliament of Religions in Chicago and goes on to found the Ramakrishna mission.
1947	Indian Independence and partition of the sub-continent into Pakistan and India.
1960-2000	Hindus from India and East Africa settle in Britain, Australia, and United States.
1964	Foundation in Delhi of Visva Hindu Parisad, the World Hindu Association.
1965	The Hare Krishna movement appears in New York; changes to U.S. immigration laws enable larger numbers of people from South Asia, including many Hindus, to come to the United States.
1972	Hindus are forced out of East Africa and settle in Britain in large numbers.
2013	Kumbha Mela at Allahabad attracts an estimated 120 million Hindus, making it the world's largest-ever religious gathering.
2017	The global Hindu population exceeds 1 billion people, with more than 2.2 million living in the United States.

Series Glossary of Key Terms

afterlife—a term that refers to a continuation of existence beyond the natural world, or after death.

BCE and CE—alternatives to the traditional Western designation of calendar eras, which used the birth of Jesus as a dividing line. BCE stands for "Before the Common Era," and is equivalent to BC ("Before Christ"). Dates labeled CE, or "Common Era," are equivalent to *Anno Domini* (AD, or "the Year of Our Lord").

chant—the rhythmic speaking or singing of words or sounds, intended to convey emotion in worship or to express the chanter's spiritual side. Chants can be conducted either on a single pitch or with a simple melody involving a limited set of notes, and often include a great deal of repetition.

creation—the beginnings of humanity, earth, life, and the universe. According to most religions, creation was a deliberate act by a supreme being.

deity (or god)—a supernatural being, usually considered to have significant power. Deities/gods are worshiped and considered sacred by human beings. Some deities are believed to control time and fate, to be the ultimate judges of human worth and behavior, and to be the designers and creators of the Earth or the universe. Others are believed to control natural phenomena, such as lightning, floods, and storms. They can assume a variety of forms, but are frequently depicted as having human or animal form, as well as specific personalities and characteristics.

hymn—a song specifically written as a song of praise, adoration or prayer, typically addressed to a god or deity.

miracle—according to many religions, a miracle is an unusual example of divine intervention in the universe by a god or deity, often one in which natural laws are overruled, suspended, or modified.

prayer—an effort to communicate with a deity or god, or another form of spiritual entity. Prayers are usually intended to offer praise, to make a request, or simply to express the person's thoughts and emotions.

prophecy—the prediction of future events, thanks to either direct or indirect communication with a deity or god. The term prophecy is also used to describe the revelation of divine will.

religion—a system of belief concerning the supernatural, sacred, or divine; and the moral codes, practices, values, institutions and rituals associated with such belief. There are many different religions in the world today.

ritual—a formal, predetermined set of symbolic actions generally performed in a particular environment at a regular, recurring interval. The actions that make up a ritual often include, but are not limited to, such things as recitation, singing, group processions, repetitive dance, and manipulation of sacred objects. The general purpose of rituals is to engage a group of people in unified worship, in order to strengthen their communal bonds.

saint—a term that refers to someone who is considered to be exceptionally virtuous and holy. It can be applied to both the living and the dead and is an acceptable term in most of the world's popular religions. A saint is held up as an example of how all other members of the religious community should act.

worship—refers to specific acts of religious praise, honor, or devotion, typically directed to a supernatural being such as a deity or god. Typical acts of worship include prayer, sacrifice, rituals, meditation, holidays and festivals, pilgrimages, hymns or psalms, the construction of temples or shrines, and the creation of idols that represent the deity.

Organizations to Contact

American Hindu Association
PO Box 628243
Middleton, WI 53562
Phone: (608) 234-8634
Email: contact.aha@aha-svtemple.org
Website: www.aha-svtemple.org

Hindu American Foundation
910 Seventeenth St. NW, Suite 316A
Washington, DC 20006
Phone: (202) 223-8222
Fax: (202) 223-8004
Website: www.hafsite.org

North American Hindu Association
9803 Goldfinch Ct
Saline, MI 48176
Phone: (612) 470-6242
Email: info@naha.us
Website: http://naha.us

Ramakrishna-Vivekananda Center
17 East 94th Street
New York, NY 10128
Phone: (212) 534-9445
Fax: (212) 828-1618
Email: rvcenternewyork@gmail.com
Website: www.ramakrishna.org

Sri Venkateswara Temple
1230 South McCully Drive
P.O. Box 17280
Penn Hills, PA 15235
Phone: (412) 373-3380
Fax: (412) 373-7650
Email: srivaru@svtemple.org
Website: www.svtemple.org

**Vedanta Society
of Southern California**
Hollywood Temple
1946 Vedanta Place
Hollywood, CA 90068
Phone: (323) 465-7114
Email: hollywood@vedanta.org
Website: https://vedanta.org

Further Reading

Swami Achuthananda. *Many Many Gods of Hinduism*. North Charleston, SC: CreateSpace, 2013.

Swami Bhaskarananda. *The Essentials of Hinduism: A Comprehensive Overview of the World's Oldest Religion*. Seattle: Viveka Press, 2002.

Bowker, John. *World Religions: The Great Faiths Explored and Explained*. London: Dorling Kindersley Ltd., 2006.

Dasi, Visakha. *Bhagavad-gita: A Photographic Essay*. Mercerville, NJ: Spiritual Journey Press, 2015.

McDermott, Gerald R. *World Religions: An Indispensable Introduction*. Nashville, Tenn.: Thomas Nelson, 2011.

Miles, Jack, et al, editors. *The Norton Anthology of World Religions*. 2 vols. New York: W.W. Norton and Co., 2014.

Pandey, Mohan R. *Hinduism: A Path to Inner Peace*. North Charleston, S.C.: CreateSpace, 2014.

Smith, Huston. *The World's Religions*. New York: HarperCollins, 2009.

Vanamali. Shiva: *Stories and Teachings from the Shiva Mahapurana*. Rochester, VT: Inner Traditions, 2013.

Internet Resources

http://aianational.com

The Association of Indians in America (AIA) is the oldest national association of Asian Indians in America. The organization concerns itself with the social welfare of South Asians who have decided to live in the United States.

www.bbc.co.uk/religion/religions/hinduism

This page from the British Broadcasting Company (BBC) provides information about Hindu beliefs, customs, history, and ethics.

www.indius.org

Indian Americans Involved in the U.S (IndiUS) is a forum created to share news and articles that promote the culture of Indian Americans and encourage community involvement.

www.iado.org

The homesite of the Indo-American Democratic Organization (IADO), a lobby group that serves Indian Americans and is engaged in issues concerning them, including immigration, education, and hate crimes.

www.newsindia-times.com

A New York–based newspaper reporting on issues of interest to the Indian community.

www.rediff.com

A media and Internet company with comprehensive resources for the Indian American community.

www.littleindia.com

A monthly feature magazine with articles on Indian life outside of India.

www.cia.gov/library/publications/the-world-factbook

The CIA World Factbook is a convenient source of basic information about any country in the world. This site includes links to a page on each country with religious, geographic, demographic, economic, and governmental data.

www.sacred-texts.com

The Internet Sacred Text Archive has an enormous repository of electronic texts about religion, mythology, legends and folklore, and occult and esoteric topics. Texts related to Hinduism include translations of the Vedas, the Bhagavad-Gita, and other primary texts.

www.pewresearch.org/topics/hindus-and-hinduism/

This page run by the Pew Research Center provides links to polls and articles about the opinions and attitudes of Hindus in the United States, as well as views of Hinduism.

Index

Numbers in ***bold italics*** refer to captions.

stages (ashrams) of life, 53–55
Swami Narayana Mission, 44

temples, *17, 40*, 56, *57, 62*
timeline, Hinduism, 100–101
transcendental meditation, 71–72
  See also meditation

Valmiki, 52
Varanasi, India, *6, 10, 11, 46*, 64, 98
varna-ashrama-dharma, 33
varnas, 20, 55
Vedas, 20, 23, 24, 25, *28*, 35, 40
  and gurus, 50, 53
vegetarianism, 35, 49, 69, 72–74
Vishnu (deity), 8, 12, 15, 27, *28*, 48, 61
  incarnations of, 14, 15, 30, *31*
  See also Krishna (deity); Rama (deity)
Visva Hindu Parisad ("World Hindu Association"), 45
Vivekananda, 42
Vyasadeva, 52

women's rights, 89–90
worship practices, 55–56, 58

Yamuna River, 64, 66, 98
Yasoda (deity), 53
yoga, 48, 58–59, 69, 70–71, 72, 76
  See also meditation

About the Author

Nalini Rangan is the daughter of South Asians who immigrated to the United Kingdom in the 1960s. A native of London, she graduated with honors from Holborne College in 1992. She has written articles for many magazines and newspapers. This is her first book for young people.